art
of a vanished race

the Mimbres Classic Black-On-White

THE AUTHORS:

Victor M. Giammattei (writer, veterinarian, teacher) and
Nanci Greer Reichert (fashion designer) are both natives of
California. As for their book, they consider it a tribute to the
forgotten people of the American Southwest.

ACKNOWLEDGEMENTS

We gratefully acknowledge the Peabody Museum of Archaeology And
Ethnology, Harvard University, for permission to render our drawings after
drawings appearing in their publication *The Swarts Ruin* by H.S. and C.B.
Cosgrove. Similarly, we extend our gratitude to the Smithsonian Institution for
permission to do the same with drawings appearing in their publications,
Additional Designs On Prehistoric Mimbres Pottery and *Designs On Prehistoric
Pottery From The Mimbres Valley, New Mexico,* both by J. Walter Fewkes.
(See each plate for specific citation.) And finally, special thanks to Mrs.
Rosemary Woodrow, librarian, for her relentless pursuit to help.

ISBN 0-944383-21-1 Third Printing - 1993

Library of Congress Catalog Card Number: 75-28600

High-Lonesome Books
P. O. Box 878
Silver City, NM 88062

By
Victor Michael Giammattei, DVM
and
Nanci Greer Reichert

DRAWINGS rendered by
Darcy Paige

art
of a vanished race

the Mimbres Classic Black-On-White

Introduction

THE MIMBRES OF THE MOGOLLON CULTURE: A People of Mystery

by Andrew Gulliford, Ph.D.

A thousand years ago the prehistoric Southwest was home to three distinct Indian cultures. The Hohokam People lived near present-day Phoenix and irrigated vast stretches of the Salt River Valley to plant cotton. The Anasazi inhabited the Colorado Plateau and built magnificent three and four story stone structures whose doorways and window openings we now know to be oriented to solar and lunar positions. In the fertile Mimbres and Gila River valleys of southwest New Mexico a completely different culture evolved which did not specialize in either large scale agriculture or massive construction projects. Instead the Mimbres people of the Mogollón Culture produced what is widely considered to be the finest prehistoric ceramic pottery in the United States, if not the world. Their timeless designs are featured in this book.

The actual artifacts can be found in the world's major museums including the Museum of Modern Art in New York City, the Heard Museum in Phoenix, the Peabody Museum of Harvard University, the Taylor Museum of the Colorado Springs Fine Arts Center, the Museum of Northern Arizona, and the Museum of Man in San Diego. In Europe the bowls can be found in collections in Paris, Copenhagen, Cambridge, Berlin, Zurich, and Stockholm. The largest permanent exhibit of Mimbres pottery is featured at the Western New Mexico University Museum in Silver City, New Mexico, in the center of the Mimbres heartland. Why the Mimbreños evolved such a distinctive and compelling black-on-white painting style remains a mystery, but now, at the end of the 20th century we are at last beginning to learn more about these extraordinary artists.

We know they traveled a great deal. A recent article published in *American Antiquity* concludes that Mimbres fish featured on 23 different prehistoric bowls render artistic interpretations of salt water fish species from the Gulf of California. Two of the bowls described in the article are displayed at the Western New Mexico University Museum and originated in the Mimbres Valley. Obviously, the Mimbres had to walk a vast distance over forbidding stretches of the Chihuahuan and Sonoran deserts to reach the Sea of Cortez.

Scientists are also starting to consider the social organization of the Mimbres people as a matriarchy. Women probably ran the villages, created the bowls and painted the intricate, flawless designs which could have been passed down from generation to generation, though the classic period of the Mimbres extended only from 900 to 1,150 A.D. After the mid-12th century the Mimbreños vanished and their art remained buried in the floors of their pueblo homes.

These bowls represent the highest expression of funerary art in the United States. The Mimbres buried their dead with the bowls on top of their heads and they ceremonially "killed" each bowl with a small hole in the center so that the deceased's spirit could arise to another world. Lost for centuries, Mimbres geometric designs and ceramic paintings of animals, insects, and mythical creatures have universal appeal. The paintings of humans show scenes of hunting, gambling, planting crops, fishing, making love and giving birth.

Because of the almost photographic nature of these realistic bowls, they are highly sought after by collectors, particularly West Germans and the Japanese. The burgeoning black market for Mimbres artifacts entices pot-hunters to rob graves in search of Mimbres bowls. Unlike most countries, including Great Britain, Greece, Columbia, Mexico, and the Soviet Union, the United States does not yet have an export law banning the international trafficking in American antiquities. Consequently, foreign investors are taking the rich prehistoric heritage of the American Southwest out of the country forever. This trafficking in grave goods must be stopped, and it is books like *Art of a Vanished Race* which offer an antidote to such cultural thievery by expertly replicating the Mimbres designs and leaving the original artifacts safe and secure in museums.

Mimbres artwork has been faithfully reproduced on these plates despite the difficulty in transferring a three dimensional design from a concave bowl to a page in a book. The authors are to be commended for the precision and accuracy of their drawings and for their concise yet revealing interpretations. *Art of a Vanished Race* is an excellent introduction to the designs of the Mimbres people, which, though prehistoric, appear very bold and contemporary. Without question, Mimbres potters created world class art.

~ ~ ~ ~ ~ ~ ~ ~ ~ ~ ~

Andrew Gulliford testified before a U.S. Senate Committee on the National Mimbres Bill and has consulted on Mimbres collections for the National Park Service. From 1987-1990 he directed the Western New Mexico University Museum. He is now Assistant Professor of History and Public Historian at Middle Tennessee State University.

The time was about A.D. 1000 and the place was the low mountain region of southwestern New Mexico and adjacent southeastern Arizona. It was then and in that region that arose a peaceable group of people whom we now refer to as the Mimbres Indians (Mimbreños). These people, though primitive in most respects, developed a refined and sophisticated hand-molded pottery, adorned with delicately finished black-on-white geometric and naturalistic designs that go unrivalled in all the 8,000 years of pottery making.

To be sure, long before A.D. 1000, actual techniques for making pottery were much further advanced in other cultures, particularly in the Old World. For example, the pottery wheel had been in use for thousands of years[1] and glazes had been applied for nearly as long. More recently, the Chinese had developed first their stoneware and then, in about A.D. 600, their remarkable porcelain that caused envy in potters throughout the Old World. The Mimbres, however, knew nothing of this.

Who were the Mimbres? What was their origin; why did they disappear? From whom did they learn their art, and why was it discontinued?

[1]By A.D. 1000, the potters wheel had been in use for at least 5,000 years, apparently first appearing in the Tigris-Euphrates River Valley with the first settlers, the Ubiad people who came from the north.

Like other prehistoric[2] men in America, they were descendants of the nomadic large-game hunters who set foot on the American continent during the last part of the Ice Age, having crossed from northern Siberia to Alaska. To get a better idea of how the Mimbres fit into the web of humanity and in order to appreciate what they accomplished in producing such refined pottery in their primitive world, it is necessary to have some idea of the development of mankind and particularly the development of the art of pottery making.

For this reason, our story begins around 50,000 years ago in those parts of the Old World where modern man, as we would recognize him, was scurrying about the countryside eking out his sustenance by hunting, fishing and gathering, and occasionally settling in natural shelters such as caves. We progress quickly through prehistory to the first of the great civilizations, then down to about the time of Christ, and finally focus on the Mimbres' direct ancestors and then on the Mimbres themselves: their life, pottery and pottery designs.

BEFORE POTTERY

Between 50,000 years ago and about the time of the first evidence of pottery (about 6500 B.C.), man was heading in a direct line to the establishment of civilizations which would soon after give rise to governments, widespread trade, monetary systems, economic controls, and large-scale warfare, and which would eventually serve as the womb for the conception of technology. Early in this period when man was inevitably preparing himself—for better or worse—for civilization, he existed in a crude, Stone Age world. Stone knife blades, projectile points, scrapers, burins and like objects comprised the bulk of his tools. Besides these, he made stone bowls as well as bone awls and even needles. He filled his stomach with large game, such as bison,

[2]The term prehistoric refers to the period before written history. In the Old World written records appear before the time of Christ, but in most areas of the New World, they did not appear until the coming of the Spanish in the late fourteen hundreds. Because of this, we may speak of the prehistoric Indians of the Southwest as late as the fourteen hundreds.

reindeer, horse, camel and cave bear which he hunted, and with an assortment of small animals and various plants which he trapped and gathered.[3] While this is a long way in time from the Mimbres, it is important in that some 50,000 years later the Mimbres are found living a similar lifestyle.

As time progressed, man became more settled and formed small villages and then larger communities. While this was occurring, a division of labor became more important, with the young men generally hunting the larger game and the women gathering small animals and plants. This division of labor allowed some individuals to spend most of their time producing single objects, such as stone tools or hunting implements, and was a necessary prerequisite for the advancement of culture and the birth of civilization.

One more element was necessary before great civilizations could emerge, namely, the domestication of some plants and animals in order to assure an adequate and continuous food supply. This occurred about the same time that man started making pottery.

While primitive man was forming larger communities and starting to produce various forms of art, small nomadic groups slowly migrated, advancing to all parts of the world. As all evidence now points, sometime between about 25,000 B.C. and 10,000 B.C. man entered the New World by crossing the Bering Strait (then a wide land mass) from Siberia to Alaska, and began to make his way very slowly through a corridor formed by the melting of the huge glaciers covering the North American continent. His trek continued down to Central and then South America, to its very tip. At about the same time, he migrated from the Old World down into Australia (by way of the now submerged Sunda Shelf which interconnected a number of Indonesian Islands) then to Tasmania, across to Polynesia and finally to New Zealand. So by no later than 10,000 B.C. man occupied the greater part of the earth.

ENTERS POTTERY

By at least 6500 B.C. the earliest pottery known to exist was being made in cave-dwelling communities in Anatolia, the western plateau lands of Turkey.[4] It was handmade from a reddish brown clay and was undecorated. Who it was that first started decorating pots will probably never be known, but by 5000 B.C. painted pottery of various designs was being made in many highland communities of Anatolia, Syria, Northern Iraq, and Turkmenia (or Turkmen, part of the USSR). Later this innovation spread along the nearby fertile river valleys in Egypt and Mesopotamia.

As centuries passed, pottery became more and more important for cooking vessels and storage containers and also as an outlet for artistic expressions and cultural notations. By about 3000 B.C. an endless variety of plain and decorated pottery was being made in most parts of the Old World—the Near, Middle and Far East, and various places in Europe and Africa. This period also marks the first appearance of pottery in the New World, in Ecuador.

By this time, the earliest and some of the greatest civilizations were flourishing. They all had arisen along major river valleys—first along the Euphrates in Iraq and the Nile in Egypt, then along the Indus in Pakistan and India, and a little later along the Hwang Ho (Yellow) River in China.

And so it went in the Old World. For the next two thousand years, many civilizations were born, grew, matured, fell and dissipated —except for a few such as the incredible Chinese civilization which has endured in essentials down to modern times. While the Old World had already witnessed the coming and going of many important civilizations, those of the New World were just coming into existence: the Olmec 1000 - 300 B.C., then the

---

[3]While the life of prehistoric man was simple, it was by no means easy. He had to contend with rapidly changing environments ushered in by glacial and interglacial periods. The drastically altered climatic conditions in turn gave rise to changes in the plant and, subsequently, animal life. While various species of plants and animals evolved, flourished, and disappeared, man constantly adapted to each new environment and the plant and animal life it offered—only because of this was he able to survive while lower members of the animal kingdom perished.

[4]The earliest evidence of any form of ceramics (long before actual pottery) comes to us from the low mountain regions of parts of Europe and Asia and dates back to between 30,000 B.C. and 20,000 B.C. Some time in this period, people of this area—called Gravettians—made small figurines of stone and of clay that had been hardened by exposure to heat. These tiny figures took the shapes of various animals, such as the mammoth, cave bear and reindeer, and perhaps even more interesting, the shapes of women, sometimes nude and most often pregnant—Venus figures as they are now called.

Teotihuacan (300 B.C. - A.D. 300), giving rise to the Mayan (A.D. 300 - 900) and later, of course, the Aztec (A.D. 900 - 1520). All of these civilizations, both in the Old and the New World, produced a vast array of interesting and enchanting plain and decorated pottery, but none with geometric and, particularly, naturalistic designs as fine and as intriguing as those of the Mimbres, who arose at this late date and who were completely ignorant of all but the simplest methods of pottery making.

ENTERS MIMBRES

By A.D. 1000, at least 8,000 years had elapsed since the first domestication of plants and animals; 5,000 years since the advent of the free-spinning pottery wheel; 4,000 years since the early dynastic phase of the great Sumerian civilization, with its wealth of metal tools, weapons, art work, and public buildings; 2,000 years since the Phoenician sea merchants had developed the first alphabet; and about 1,400 years since Socrates, Plato, and then Aristotle had given the world a philosophy that would shape western man's thinking for millennia to come. After mankind had experienced all of this, and much more, then enter the Mimbres Indians, who made simple stone implements; who lived in crude houses with walls of stacked, unshaped river-boulders plastered with mud; who ate wild rabbits, antelope, small rodents and an assortment of wild and cultivated plants; who buried their dead a few inches under the packed adobe floors in their houses; and who knew nothing of the wheel in any form—but who did make an incredible pottery.

While the critics of prehistoric Southwestern Indians are quick to point out their primitiveness, they sometimes forget the conditions of the environment in which they lived. North, Central and South America for the most part had relatively few plants and animals suitable for domestication and cultivation. There was no wheat, eikorn, barley, or emmer; there were no oxen, goats, pigs, sheep or horses. The people knew nothing of the wheel, nor would it have done them much good without suitable animals to pull carts or wagons. They had no extensive fertile river valleys such as the Euphrates, Nile, Indus, or Hwang Ho of the Old World. Some say that for the Mimbres to have produced such sophisticated pottery in the short span of 200 years was an almost impossible feat; but if we take a close look, we see that their pottery evolved over nearly a millennium with direct influence from the Mogollon (their predecessors) and indirect influence from their western neighbors, the Hohokam, and from their northern neighbors, the Anasazi people.[5]

[5]From about the time of Christ to about A.D. 1000, the Mogollon (the Mountain People, predecessors to the Mimbres), the Hohokam (the Desert People), and the Anasazi (first, the Basket-Makers and later the Pueblo Indians) existed side-by-side in the great Southwestern Basin. The Mogollon territory extended from the low arid regions of northern Chihuahua, Mexico, to the higher, moist mountain areas in southwestern New Mexico and adjacent southeastern Arizona. The Hohokam occupied the desert country extending from northern Sonora, Mexico, to central and southern Arizona. The Anasazi inhabited much of the high plateau country of the four corners states (Arizona, Utah, Colorado, and New Mexico). Besides these territorial distinctions, cultural distinctions are also evident. The Hohokam, for example, cremated their dead, while the Mogollon buried theirs, mainly in a flexed or semi-flexed position and, near the end of their era, usually in the earth floors of their houses. The Anasazi buried their dead in a similar position but outside of their houses. This kind of evidence, along with the evidence of trade, supports the idea that the Mogollon, the Hohokam, and the Anasazi were three separate and distinct cultures which occurred in the same general area and which interacted with one another.

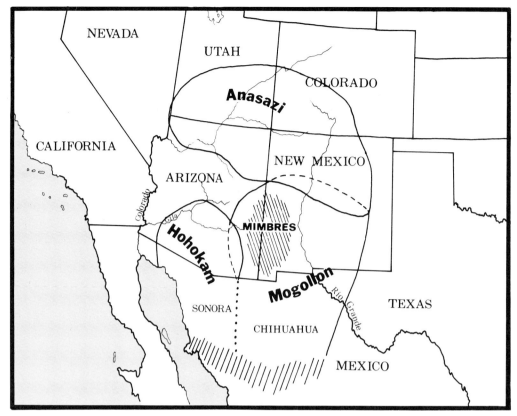

§Adapted from (1) Gordon R. Willey, *An Introduction to American Archaeology*. (2) Erik K. Reed, "Trends in Southwestern Archeology." (See Sources, page 15)

MIMBRES' HERITAGE

The Mimbres arose from the Mogollon, who in turn had arisen from the Cochise—all three groups having occupied nearly the same territory, but at different times. The evolution of these groups was accompanied by a slow, northerly migration that ended thousands of years later with the Mimbres occupying only southwestern New Mexico and adjacent southeastern Arizona.

THE COCHISE   These sedentary people (probably direct descendants of the large-game hunters of the Old World) most likely lived by camping along the edges of streams where they hunted an assortment of animals and gathered seeds which they ground on simple milling stones. They did little farming and produced no pottery nor permanent houses. They retained this primitive life-style for thousands of years with relatively no change, eventually fading away, giving rise to the Mogollon culture, the beginning of which is marked by the first appearance of permanent subterranean houses, pottery and a greater reliance on agriculture.

THE MOGOLLON   The early Mogollon lived in crude, unconnected, round, subterranean pit-houses with earth walls and floors and low earth-covered roofs supported by small logs, branches and twigs. As time progressed, houses were built closer to ground level; they took on a rectangular shape, and simple masonry was employed. Early Mogollon subsisted by collecting seeds, nuts, roots, bulbs, berries, insects, and small rodents. They hunted very little, and cultivated relatively small amounts of maize, beans and squash, which increased as time progressed. Initially, they produced simple, undecorated brown pottery and it was not until nearly A.D. 700 that the first painted designs appeared on Mogollon pots—possibly the result of influence from their Hohokam neighbors to the west, who had apparently been painting pottery since nearly the time of Christ. The Mogollon's tools consisted of an assortment of stone and bone implements, many similar to those of ancient man of 50,000 and 100,000 years ago, and were virtually the same as those of their predecessors, though they did produce more stones for the milling and grinding of seeds.

Two important innovations mark what was probably the peak of the Mogollon era: the first was Boldfaced Black-On-White pottery which preceded the more refined Classic Black-On-White pottery (both of which are thin walled, white pots with painted black designs). The second innovation was the crude stone ax. Other than this, little change occurred throughout the Mogollon era (300 B.C. - A.D. 1000) except near the end, with the appearance of rough-surfaced Corrugated pottery (brown pottery with a ripply exterior), and ground level dwellings. These new houses also differed in that they were built with plastered, stacked stone walls adjoining one another, forming networks of interconnecting rooms (pueblo style).[6] These changes, first in pottery and then in housing, mark the fading of the Mogollon and the blossoming of the Mimbres—at around A.D. 1000.

While the preceding information helps clarify the origin of the Mimbres themselves and indicates some of the influences on their pottery, it reveals little about what the Mimbres were like as a people—how they lived from day to day, what they thought. Because they did not leave any form of written record, we can answer such questions only by speculating on the significance of archaeological evidence, such as their decorated pottery, and by studying those Indians who lived in the same locale but several centuries later and for whom recorded information does exist.[7]

Because it would be impossible to establish a complete picture of the Mimbres culture, we will outline only small vignettes of their way of life and some of their beliefs. We will do this while discussing their method of pottery production and their unique designs.

MIMBRES POTTERY

In 1932, Alfred Kidder, the eminent archaeologist of the American Southwest, commenting on the Mimbres and their Classic Black-On-White pottery, said:

> . . . in the making of pottery they stood unrivalled and supreme. No ware of the Southwest can approach that of the Mimbres either in technical perfection of brushwork, or in the variety, freedom, and sheer boldness of its decorative conception. It is amazing stuff.[8]

At about the same time, Paul Nesbitt, who did some classical archaeological work in the Mimbres Valley, stated it another way:

> The houses and stone implements of the Mimbreños were the simplest, yet for keenness of observation in observing animal and bird life and in ingenuity of producing these by means of paint on pottery, the Mimbreños were the most unique of all Southwest potters. As for the designs on geometric bowls, one almost becomes lost in admirations of their variety and beauty. Of the larger number of geometric bowls found, no two are alike . . .[9]

Indeed, the Mimbres did produce an amazing pottery. Not only does it go unrivalled in the Southwest, but to some degree throughout the world—partly in the formation of the bowls but mainly in the incredibly refined and sophisticated hand-painted designs, particularly those unique animal characterizations. Nothing like these exist in the world, prehistoric or otherwise.

Though this remarkable pottery seems to have appeared overnight during the tenth century A.D., its origin rests in at least a thousand years of development which saw innumerable forms, styles, adornments, and eventually painted designs—all of which had outside influences, particularly from the neighboring Hohokam and Anasazi peoples. To avoid a lengthy, detailed explanation of this development, tracing it through a thousand years of pottery making, the salient features have been condensed and are presented in

---

[6]These changes in house style and construction were probably influenced by the Anasazi people to the north who had been building and living in such pueblo type villages for centuries.

[7]Up to 75 years ago, the Pueblo Indian culture of the surrounding area had changed little since the time of Columbus. It seems within reason, therefore, to assume that the Mimbres culture (300 years before Columbus) was little different from the culture of those Indians whom the early explorers encountered in these same regions and for whom records exist.

[8]From Alfred Kidder's "Introduction" to H.S. and C.B. Cosgrove's book, The Swarts Ruin, p. XX. (See Sources, page 15).

[9]From Paul H. Nesbitt, The Ancient Mimbreños, p. 55. (See Sources, page 15)

Fig. 2 Development of the Mogollon-Mimbres, Hohokam and Anasazi Cultures with Notations of Pottery Development§

ESTIMATED DATES	CULTURES		
	MOGOLLON – mimbres	HOHOKAM	ANASAZI
300 B.C.	**Mogollon I** Three types of undecorated pottery	PIONEER at least seven varieties of pottery were produced of which four were painted geometric designs predominanted	BASKET MAKER I
100 B.C.			
BIRTH OF CHRIST			
A.D. 100			BASKET MAKER II
A.D. 300	**Mogollon II** Red – on – Brown Red – on – White first painted pottery geometric designs		BASKET MAKER III beginning of pottery
A.D. 500		COLONIAL	
A.D. 700	**Mogollon III IV and V** first Boldfaced Black-On-White		PUEBLO I Black-on-White pottery being produced
A.D. 900			
A.D. 1050	first Classic Black-On-White **Mimbres**	SEDENTARY	PUEBLO II
A.D. 1150		CLASSIC	PUEBLO III

§Adapted from (1) Paul S. Martin, George I. Quimby, and Donald Collier, *Indians Before Columbus.* (2) C.W. Ceram, *The First American.* (3) Gordon R. Willey, *An Introduction to American Archaeology* (See Sources, page 15)

Figures 2 and 3. From these figures the reader may quickly grasp the chronological sequence of pottery production leading to the Mimbres Classic Black-On-White Ware and gain some understanding of the possible Hohokam and Anasazi influences.

As indicated, many forms of pottery were made by the Mimbres, but for the rest of this discussion, all descriptions and remarks about their pottery and designs will refer only to the Mimbres Classic Black-On-White Ware.

FORMING THE BOWLS

Each bowl was made by a coiling process, generally from one long thin roll of clay. The potter (apparently women as some evidence suggests) took a chunk of clay and rolled it out, making a long thin roll. Then, starting with one end as the very center and bottom of the bowl, she coiled the roll around and upon itself, first expanding the bottom and then raising the sides, working the coils to get the desired dimensions and shape. Most bowls recovered averaged between 7 and 11 inches in diameter and about 5 inches in depth. The shapes vary from round bottomed, nearly hemispherical (which predominate) to flat bottomed, flowerpot shaped.

In forming the bowl, the corrugated sides of the freshly coiled clay were smoothed over by taking a scraping tool (such as an old piece of ceramic or stone scraper) and working it back and forth over the inside and outside of the bowl. Now it was ready for burnishing. This was done by rubbing a smooth stone over its inner and outer surfaces, thus working the rough particles in deep and bringing the smooth ones to the surface—much like finishing concrete with a trowel. The bowl was air-dried for a period, then a white slip (a creamy suspension of clay) was applied to all surfaces. It was then left to air-dry again, then reburnished. The bowl was now ready for painting.

POTTERY PAINT

The paint was black and was composed of a carbonaceous material and iron oxide. Most likely it was made (as it was some time later by early Pueblo Indians) by preparing extracts from the Mustard or Guaco (Bee) plant. Shortly after these plants had bloomed in the spring, the women pulled them up, left them to dry and then stored them. To get the black material, the dried plants were boiled for several hours, then the fibrous material was removed and the liquid was left to boil until it became black, thick and syrupy. This was cooled, then poured into containers, such as corn husks, and left to dry in the sun for a number of days until it had hardened, forming dried cakes. It could then be stored indefinitely.

Fig. 3 Development and Disappearance of Mogollon-Mimbres Pottery Types§

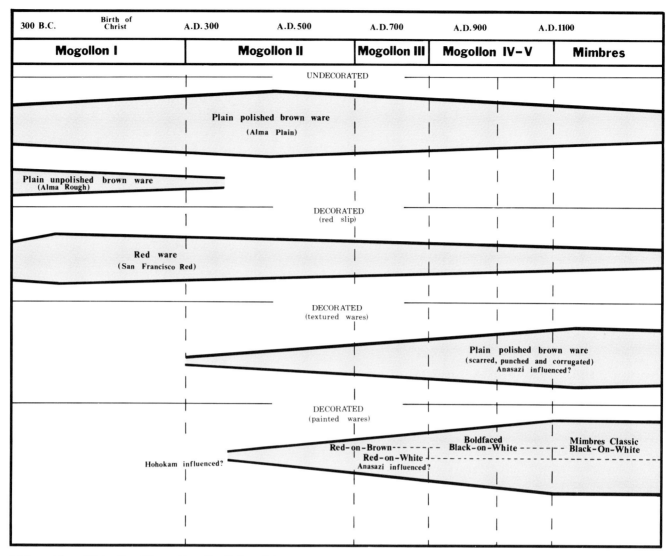

§Adapted from (1) Joe Ben Wheat, *Mogollon Culture Prior to A.D. 1000* (2) Paul S. Martin, John B. Rinaldo, and Eloise R. Barter, *Late Mogollon Communities*. (3) Paul S. Martin, George I. Quimby, and Donald Collier, *Indians Before Columbus*. (See Sources, page 15)

To prepare the paint, flakes were scraped away from a dried cake onto a small stone palate, some water was added to liquify it and then a hematite stone was rubbed back and forth in this until enough iron oxide had ground off, making the solution a thick gravylike consistency. The paint was then ready to apply with various sized brushes that were made from yucca leaves with the fibers shredded out at one end for bristles. It is in the painting that the Mimbres achieved an unimaginable skill; their deft, unshakable hands moved rhythmically and precisely over the inner contours of the bowls, (See Plate 1) achieving such remarkable detail as a concentric border of 15 evenly spaced parallel lines, all within a width of 11/16 of an inch.

FIRING THE BOWLS

How these potters fired their ceramics is a mystery. Several things are certain, however. First, in order to get the type of ceramics they did, they had to be fired at a fairly high temperature and, second, for the painted designs to have remained dark and unfaded through firing, the bowls could not have been exposed to oxygen in the open atmosphere. In other words, they had to have been fired in some kind of smoldering fire devoid of most oxygen. They may have accomplished this as the later Pueblo Indians did, by stacking the painted unfired pots on a pile of combustible material and then covering them with more, forming a kind of blanket over the top. The kindling material underneath was then ignited and the pile left to smolder, burning itself out in time. While the post-Columbian Indians used dung from horses and cows for this purpose, it was unavailable to the Mimbres.

POTTERY DESIGNS

While the Mimbres potters reached an amazing technical skill in applying their designs it is the designs themselves which reflect their genius and creativity. Through these designs, we are allowed glimpses of their world—their impression of life, their association with nature, their lifestyle.

In reviewing the designs appearing on a vast number of bowls collected over the years, mainly two distinct categories emerge: naturalistic (those of animals, man or plants) and purely geometric.

GEOMETRIC DESIGNS

In the geometric designs we see an incredible variety with no two being identical and most evoking different emotions. In fact, frequently two designs may incorporate similar elements, yet one will evoke an aura of calm, while the other appears charged and emits explosive energy. The geometric designs range from those composed of large bold, black patterns on white, conveying a harshness, to those composed of similar bold elements but softened by delicate, lacy lines often so detailed and complex that only careful study reveals all

FIG. 4   after Figure 133, *Designs On Prehistoric Pottery From The Mimbres Valley, New Mexico*, J. Walter Fewkes, Smithsonian Miscellaneous Collection, Vol. 74, No. 6, Smithsonian Institution.

FIG. 5   after Plate 221, Figure a, *The Swarts Ruin: A Typical Mimbres Site In Southwestern New Mexico*, H.S. and C.B. Cosgrove, Vol. XV, No. 1, Peabody Museum Of American Archaeology And Ethnology.

of their facets. That these artisans could create such an uncanny harmony while combining dissimilar geometric elements is seen in Figure 4. Notice how the dark bold lines are masterfully complemented and quieted by the undulating curves. Such versatility and wide range of purely geometric designs could have arisen only from a free, innocent imagination.

NATURALISTIC DESIGNS

In their naturalistic designs, unique facets of their culture come to light, outstandingly, their close and harmonious existence with nature. One look at the charging ram in Figure 5, and one cannot help but feel the movement, the excitement, the unfettered energy surging forth. So subtly capturing such a typical animal movement and posture highlights many of the naturalistic designs of the Mimbres. To observe animal behavior, gain a feeling for it, and then to translate it onto the convex inner surface of a bowl, could have been achieved only by skilled artists living very closely with nature and having become imbued with the beauty of her creatures.

In the same vein, a definite respect and unfearful attitude glows from many animal characters depicted as friendly but serene— rarely is an animal drawn in a savage or desecrated manner, belittling its very existence. There is no butchery, no dominating or controlling, but rather peaceful coexistence. This feeling is nicely conveyed in Figure 6 in which the two men are attempting to pull a bear along by ropes. Notice the bear—no agony or pain is apparent, just a bear naturally and stubbornly resisting.

FIG. 6   after Figure 16, *Designs On Prehistoric Pottery From The Mimbres Valley, New Mexico,* J. Walter Fewkes, Smithsonian Miscellaneous Collection, Vol. 74, No. 6, Smithsonian Institution.

This same illustration also points out another outstanding feature of the Mimbres culture, that is, their apparent lack of self-interest, evidenced here by the limited and plain representation of the human figures, with little or no attention to facial or other structural elements. (See also Plates 10 and 30.)

These vaguely represented, ill-proportioned human forms (appearing on a number of bowls) are in sharp contrast with the numerous, exactingly detailed animal forms. One gains little feeling for movement or mood when viewing the human forms. This, too, is in sharp contrast to many of the animal designs. It is as though they didn't care about their own moods or feelings, but did for those of the animals.

Why this lack of self-interest? The talent was there; had they wanted, they certainly could have painted humans as skillfully as animals. There does not appear to have been a taboo on painting human figures. What then? Perhaps they concentrated on animals and not humans because of the importance animals had in their lifestyle. We must remember that it was not another human who provided the food necessary for subsistence, but rather an animal. And these were not raised and cared for by humans; they were wild and were taken by hunting, trapping or fishing. Interestingly, very few designs recovered depict these acts. In addition, though cultivated plants must have been important to the Mimbres, few designs are based on plant forms or related natural phenomena, such as the sun and rain.

In terms of pure artistry of design, the Mimbres developed two outstanding techniques in their naturalistic art which rarely occurred among primitive people. First is the utilization of a negative image and second is the creation of a feeling of the third dimension in a subject placed on a single plane surface.

The use of negative imagery is beautifully illustrated in Figures 7A and 7B. The negative images, the white rabbits, were formed by filling in the black background. This is in direct contrast to the rabbits illustrated in Figure 7B, which are positive images, having been drawn with black on the white background.

We must emphasize here that the natural approach is to draw positive images, by drawing a figure with a color, such as black, on a different colored background, such as white. To do the reverse, that is to fill in the background and create negative images,

FIG. 7A   after Figure 25, *Designs On Prehistoric Pottery From The Mimbres Valley, New Mexico,* J. Walter Fewkes, Smithsonian Miscellaneous Collection, Vol. 74, No. 6, Smithsonian Institution.

FIG. 7B   after Figure 22, *Designs On Prehistoric Pottery From The Mimbres Valley, New Mexico,* J. Walter Fewkes, Smithsonian Miscellaneous Collection, Vol. 74, No. 6, Smithsonian Institution.

FIG. 8A.   after Plate 215, Figure a, *The Swarts Ruin: A Typical Mimbres Site In Southwestern New Mexico,* H.S. and C.B. Cosgrove, Vol. XV, No. 1, Peabody Museum Of American Archaeology And Ethnology.

FIG. 8B   after Figure 29, *Additional Designs On Prehistoric Mimbres Pottery,* J. Walter Fewkes, Smithsonian Miscellaneous Collection, Vol. 76, No. 8, Smithsonian Institution.

requires an abstraction, a more sophisticated interpretation. The artist must maintain the silhouette of the positive image in his mind, mentally placing it on a drawing medium (in the case of the Mimbres, the interior of the white bowl), and then he must draw or paint in the background around it, leaving the undrawn portion as the figure desired. For the Mimbres to have mastered this is truly remarkable.

The second outstanding artistic technique they achieved (the third dimension on a single plane surface) can be seen in Figures 8A and 8B. Both are profiles of quail in natural positions, and both give a subtle feeling of the third dimension. This was done by capturing the bird's natural movements, for example in Figure 8B, the movement of the quail's head as it rotated and assumed a cocked position. Capturing this kind of natural movement and keeping it alive when translating it onto a single plane surface is a very difficult and sophisticated artistic achievement mastered by few primitive artists. Even the ancient Egyptians—far from being primitive— through many hundreds of years of producing refined art never became masters of this.

All of the designs, the naturalistic, and the geometric, take on a completely mystifying appeal when you stop and recall that they were produced by a very primitive people who had no precision tools. The Mimbres Classic Black-On-White pottery, as Alfred Kidder said, "is amazing stuff".

EXIT MIMBRES

While it is possible that the Mimbres were driven away from their villages by some barbaric warmongers from another region and while it is possible that they may have been wiped out by an epidemic, archaeological evidence does not support either of these theories. No skeletal remains show signs of being injured by weapons, no dwellings show signs of being quickly adandoned, nor villages being burned or destroyed. Similarly, there is no evidence of a catastrophic disease—no single burial sites with multiple skeletal remains nor any great increase in burials for any one given period (indicating an elevated death rate).

To the contrary, most evidence points to a slow depopulation of many of the villages. For example, houses were left undamaged and empty. Often few artifacts were found in the houses themselves; most that were recovered (such as jewelry, pots and tools) were found in burial sites along with skeletal remains. And food storage bins, for the most part, were left empty. All of this points to a planned and slow withdrawal from the area.

Well then, where did they go? Some anthropologists today believe that the Mimbres perished because of a long drought. It is well established by astronomical evidence, along with evidence gained by the study of tree rings, that a severe drought occured for 23 years, between A.D. 1276 and 1299, in the southwestern region that had served as the Mimbres' home. Further supporting this theory is that the exodus of the Mimbres from their villages has been dated to around A.D. 1300. It seems reasonable that 23 years of drought in this already arid region would be enough to drive out rattlesnakes, much less a group of people dependent on the paltry water supply of the tiny rivers in the area.

While this suggests a possible reason for the dispersal of the Mimbres, it gives no clues as to why their art of pottery was discontinued. If the Mimbres did migrate northerly, easterly or westerly, why is it that no evidence of their classical pottery appears in any new regions at a later date? As with the disappearance of any outstanding art form, it probably died with the few individuals or generations of individuals who had conceived and mastered it. One author felt that the Mimbres Classic Black-On-White Ware was probably the work of one great artist and her followers. Whatever the case, it is understandable that subsequent generations would go on to create something new, something considered their own. And, after all, in terms of the duration of the history of mankind, are not all art movements ephemeral?

SOURCES

Ceram, C.W. *The First American: A Story of North American Archaeology.* New York: Harcourt, Brace, Jovanovich, Inc., 1971.

Clark, Grahame. *World Prehistory: A New Outline.* Cambridge, Eng.: at the University Press, 1969.

Cooper, Emmanuel. *A History of Pottery.* London: Longman Group Limited London, 1972.

Cosgrove, H.S. and C.B. *The Swarts Ruin: A Typical Mimbres Site In Southwestern New Mexico.* Cambridge, Mass.: Peabody Museum Of American Archaeology And Ethnology, Harvard University, 1932.

Fewkes, J. Walter. *Designs On Prehistoric Pottery From The Mimbres Valley, New Mexico.* Smithsonian Miscellaneous Collections, Vol. 74, No. 6. Washington, D.C.: The Smithsonian Institution, 1923.

Fewkes, J. Walter. *Additional Designs On Prehistoric Mimbres Pottery.* Smithsonian Miscellaneous Collections, Vol. 76, No. 8, Washington, D.C.: The Smithsonian Institution, 1923.

Hawley, Florence M. "Prehistoric Pottery Pigments In The Southwest. "*American Anthropologist, N.S.,* Vol. 32. No. 4, pp. 731-754, 1929.

Kidder, Alfred Vincent. *An Introduction to the Study of Southwestern Archaeology: With A Preliminary Account Of Excavations At Pecos.* New Haven: Yale University Press, 1924.

Martin, Paul S.; Quimby, George I.; and Collier, Donald. *Indians Before Columbus: Twenty Thousand Years of North American History Revealed by Archaeology.* Chicago: University of Chicago Press, 1947.

Martin, Paul S.; Rinaldo, John B.; and Barter, Eloise R. *Late Mogollon Communities: Four Sites of the Tularosa Phase Western New Mexico.* Fieldiana: Anthropology, Vol. 49. No. 1. Chicago Natural History Museum, 1957.

Nesbitt, Paul H. *The Ancient Mimbreños.* Beloit, Wis.: The Logan Museum, Beloit College, 1931.

Reed, Erik K. "Trends in Southwestern Archeology." *New Interpretations of Aboriginal American Culture History.* 75th Anniversary Volume of the Anthropological Society of Washington, pp. 46-58. New York: Cooper Square Publishers, Inc., 1972.

Wheat, Joe Ben. *Mogollon Culture Prior to A.D. 1000.* American Anthropological Association, Vol. 57, No. 2, Part 3, Memoir No. 82. April, 1955.

Willey, Gordon R. *An Introduction to American Archaeology: North and Middle America.* Vol. one. Englewood Cliffs, N.J.: Prentice-Hall, Inc., 1966.

PLATE 1   This Classic Black-On-White ceramic bowl is representative of many recovered from Mimbres' grave sites. Notice the hole in its center: As part of the burial ritual, these people placed bowls along with their corpses, but when so doing, "killed" the bowls, that is punched a hole in their centers frequently shattering them. The above bowl was made sometime around A.D. 1100 - 1200.   (Photograph, courtesy of The Peabody Museum, Harvard University.

PLATE 2 *Swirling entwining spirals, reminiscent of Greek and Roman fretwork, bring to mind the amazing likenesses of many Mimbres' design elements to prior art forms. While the Mimbres artisan delighted in combining graceful fluid curves for her own pleasure, she had no idea that similar forms had delighted men centuries before.*

after Plate 148, Figure c, *The Swarts Ruin: A Typical Mimbres Site In Southwestern New Mexico,* H.S. and C.B. Cosgrove, Vol. XV, No. 1, Peabody Museum Of American Archaeology And Ethnology.

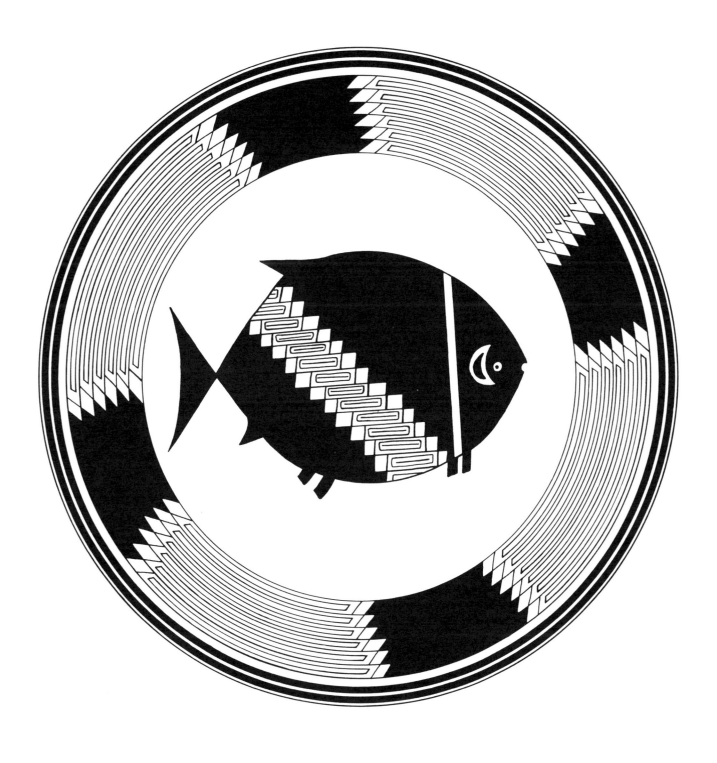

PLATE 3   By incorporating the diagonal design features of the fish in a slightly different form in the circular border, the Mimbres artist unifies these two distinct parts of the design. In a highly stylized form, the artist has indicated one of the most vital portions of fish anatomy—the gill. Were the Mimbres aware of its function?

after Plate 205, Figure c, *The Swarts Ruin: A Typical Mimbres Site in Southwestern New Mexico,* H.S. and C.B. Cosgrove, Vol. XV, No. 1, Peabody Museum Of American Archaeology And Ethnology.

PLATE 4   *Is it that the Mimbres actually observed such behavior between these newt-like creatures and the impressive bird, or is a lost legend being told? In many designs, the Mimbres painted this mouth-to-mouth relationship between various animals. Did this have special significance to them?*

after Figure 35, *Designs On Prehistoric Pottery From The Mimbres Valley, New Mexico,* J. Walter Fewkes, Smithsonian Miscellaneous Collection, Vol. 74, No. 6, Smithsonian Institution.

PLATE 5   An overwhelming feeling of force emanates from this geometric design
as the central S-shaped bar appears to have just been squeezed into shape by the
clamping jaws on either side. Transmitting such a feeling of power, energy or
movement is an outstanding accomplishment, repeated over and over again in
Mimbres painted designs (An example of the earlier Boldfaced Black-On-White
designs).

after Plate 113, Figure f, *The Swarts Ruin: A Typical Mimbres Site in Southwestern New Mexico,* H.S. and C.B. Cosgrove, Vol. XV, No. 1, Peabody Museum Of American Archaeology And Ethnology.

PLATE 6   *While this jackrabbit design is not one of the more graceful animal interpretations that the Mimbres painted, it embodies a certain innocent charm. The front feet appear buckled under, which gives the rabbit an awkward posture. Also notice the triangular shaped ears; this is a subtle feature of jackrabbit (a hare) ears which differs from the more rounded ear tips of other types of rabbits.*

after Figure 21, *Designs On Prehistoric Pottery From The Mimbres Valley, New Mexico,* J. Walter Fewkes, Smithsonian Miscellaneous Collection, Vol. 74, No. 6, Smithsonian Institution.

PLATE 7   *Emerging from the border and reflecting one another, the winged birds seem to be feeding from a flower. The wide radiating blossom is reminiscent of a sunflower. But the birds' long beaks give a clue that they are not seed eaters.*

after Figure 50, *Designs On Prehistoric Pottery From The Mimbres Valley, New Mexico,* J. Walter Fewkes, Smithsonian Miscellaneous Collection, Vol. 74, No. 6, Smithsonian Institution.

PLATE 8   The motion of a sphere throwing off parts of its mass with each revolution can be interpreted from this Mimbres geometric design. Were the Mimbres somehow conceptualizing the movement of the heavens? Are the small crosses stylized stars?

after Plate 143, Figure c, *The Swarts Ruin: A Typical Mimbres Site In Southwestern New Mexico,* H.S. and C.B. Cosgrove, Vol. XV, No. 1, Peabody Museum Of American Archaeology And Ethnology.

PLATE 9   *The sinister birds share in picking the fish bones clean and there is little doubt that the artist wished to convey an eerie mood. A skilled mood-maker, the artist cleverly achieved this by simply drawing the birds with elongated, undulating necks and with piercing evil eyes. Compare these birds with the innocence of the birds in Plate 7.*

after Figure 38, *Designs On Prehistoric Pottery From The Mimbres Valley, New Mexico,* J. Walter Fewkes, Smithsonian Miscellaneous Collection, Vol. 74, No. 6, Smithsonian Institution.

PLATE 10   The balance of nature? Interestingly, the Mimbres did understand the
concept of actually making a mobile function. The heavier weight of the fox on the
short extension is balanced by the lighter weight fish on the longer extension. In
this design, as in many others, the bodies of the animals display far more
decoration than that of the man—here definitely a man, as shown by the subtle
representation of a sexual organ.

after Plate 228, Figure e, The Swarts Ruin: A Typical
Mimbres Site In Southwestern New Mexico, H.S. and
C.B. Cosgrove, Vol. XV, No. 1, Peabody Museum Of
American Archaeology And Ethnology.

PLATE 11   *A favorite Mimbres subject, the quail assumes greatly varying postures in Mimbres art. Icy New Mexico winter air may be the reason for this quail's posture, drawing its head and tail in close to its body, seemingly trying to conserve its body heat. An abundance of birds—allowing continued observation—may be the reason for the Mimbres acute empathy with the quail.*

after Plate 215, Figure c, *The Swarts Ruin: A Typical Mimbres Site In Southwestern New Mexico,* H.S. and C.B. Cosgrove, Vol. XV, No. 1, Peabody Museum Of American Archaeology And Ethnology.

PLATE 12   *Meandering, graceful necks and legs intertwine to form a beautifully creative design unit. The amazing transformation of two simple bird images into a flowing cohesive motif truly manifests the masterful Mimbres art. All of the lines of this design work and move together, complementing over and over again the central image. The geometric shapes surrounding the elegant birds heighten the drama of their union, all of which create a unified and balanced design, inseparable from the pottery piece.*

after Figure 55, *Designs On Prehistoric Pottery From The Mimbres Valley, New Mexico,* J. Walter Fewkes, Smithsonian Miscellaneous Collection, Vol. 74, No. 6, Smithsonian Institution.

PLATE 13   *A twinkling star? Did the Mimbres conceptualize celestial phenomena?*

after Plate 142, Figure e, *The Swarts Ruin: A Typical Mimbres Site In Southwestern New Mexico*, H.S. and C.B. Cosgrove, Vol. XV, No. 1, Peabody Museum Of American Archaeology And Ethnology.

PLATE 14   Is the turtle actually swimming in the bottom of the bowl? The extended
neck and sweeping legs give the impression that this turtle has been stopped at
the very moment of a vigorous swimming stroke. Stopping natural animal action
rather than depicting a stilted pose is an incredibly difficult artistic device,
masterfully repeated by the Mimbres in many naturalistic designs.

after Plate 202, Figure d, *The Swarts Ruin: A Typical
Mimbres Site In Southwestern New Mexico,* H.S. and
C.B. Cosgrove, Vol. XV, No. 1, Peabody Museum Of
American Archaeology And Ethnology.

PLATE 15   *Two antelope silhouetted against a horizon. Probably a fairly common sight to the Mimbres.*

after Plate 224, Figure d, *The Swarts Ruin: A Typical Mimbres Site In Southwestern New Mexico,* H.S. and C.B. Cosgrove, Vol. XV, No. 1, Peabody Museum Of American Archaeology And Ethnology.

PLATE 16   Also masters of asymmetry, the Mimbres brought to their designs
pleasing proportions through the use of balanced yet unlike areas. Though this
design cannot be divided equally in half in any direction, the larger upper shapes
are complemented and balanced by the weight and proportions of the lower
shapes. This design is one of the best examples of asymmetry produced by the
Mimbres.

after Plate 157, Figure c, *The Swarts Ruin: A Typical
Mimbres Site In Southwestern New Mexico,* H.S. and
C.B. Cosgrove, Vol. XV, No. 1, Peabody Museum Of
American Archaeology And Ethnology.

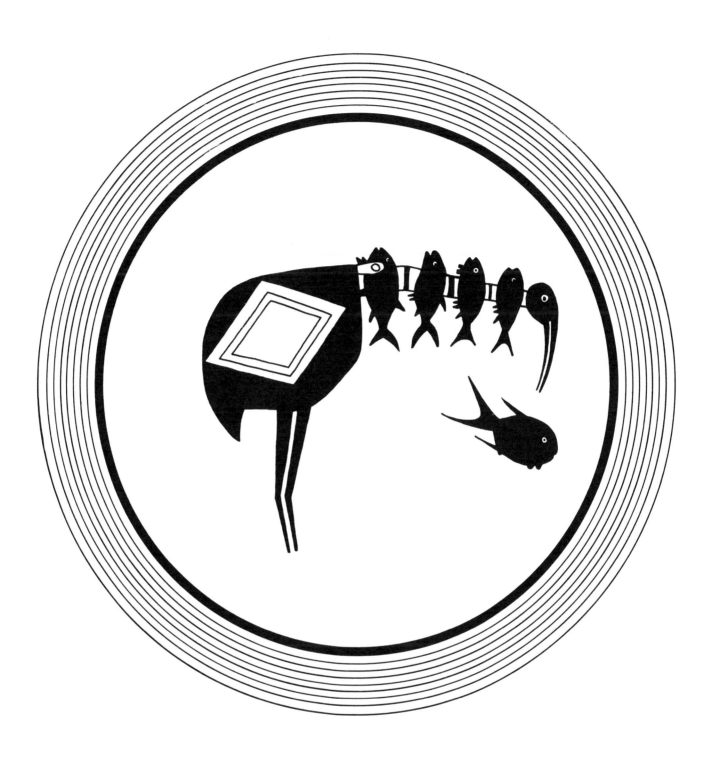

PLATE 17   *Apparently a shore bird enjoying its prey; this naturalistic design imaginatively translates two vital processes—capturing and devouring—into a single image. A subtle suggestion of the bird fishing in shallow water is conveyed by not painting in the feet.*

after Figure 26, *Additional Designs On Prehistoric Mimbres Pottery,* J. Walter Fewkes, Smithsonian Miscellaneous Collection, Vol. 76, No. 8, Smithsonian Institution.

PLATE 18   *Fanciful, rather than deadly, this elaborately adorned scorpion points
to the Mimbres fearless approach to nature. Through the elaborate decoration of
the body, regard rather than dread is portrayed.*

after Plate 198, Figure e, *The Swarts Ruin: A Typical
Mimbres Site In Southwestern New Mexico,* H.S. and
C.B. Cosgrove, Vol. XV, No. 1, Peabody Museum Of
American Archaeology And Ethnology.

PLATE 19   *The checkerboard of black-on-white (a favorite Mimbres design element, found in varying forms in both naturalistic and geometric designs) is incorporated throughout this intricate geometric maze. The checkerboard dramatically points out the Mimbres skillful brushwork and their imaginative variations of a single design element.*

after Plate 133, Figure f, *The Swarts Ruin: A Typical Mimbres Site In Southwestern New Mexico,* H.S. and C.B. Cosgrove, Vol. XV, No. 1, Peabody Museum Of American Archaeology And Ethnology.

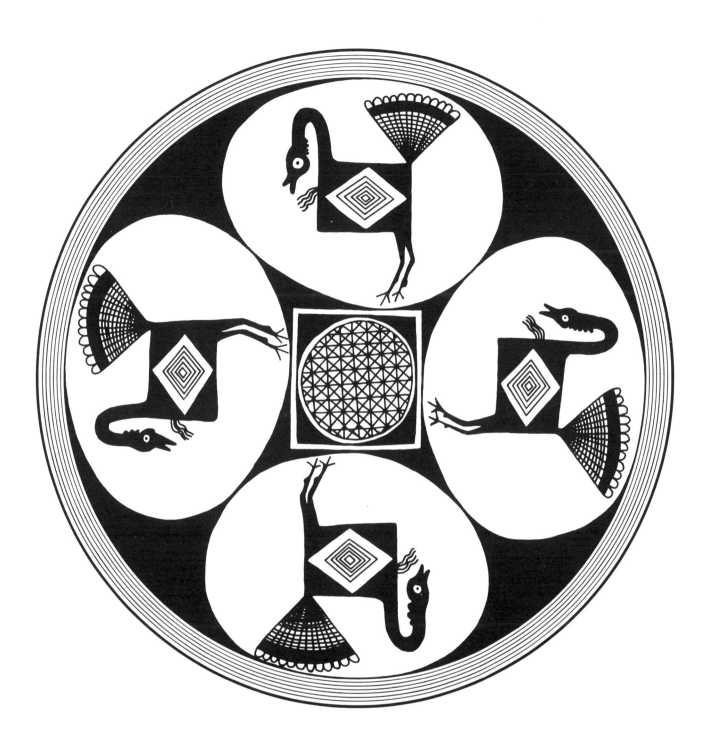

PLATE 20   *Are the Mimbres illustrating the concept of the progression of life by encasing the refined turkeys in eggshapes from which they once emerged? It may be possible that the Mimbres artist had this image in mind, or rather that this is a way of highlighting an animal held in esteem. There is evidence to support the latter as the Mimbres apparently kept domesticated turkeys, yet very few bones were found in refuse areas, possibly indicating that they worshipped the animals and did not eat them.*

after Plate 216, Figure d, *The Swarts Ruin: A Typical Mimbres Site In Southwestern New Mexico,* H.S. and C.B. Cosgrove, Vol. XV, No. 1, Peabody Museum Of American Archaeology And Ethnology.

PLATE 21   Austerely simplistic, this extremely unusual Mimbres design almost
appears unfinished. Has the man been speared to the side of the bowl or is that an
unfinished arm extending outward? His face does not show any agonizing
expression, yet the unnatural position of his legs does make him appear to be
nailed to the side of the bowl.

after Plate 227, Figure a, *The Swarts Ruin: A Typical
Mimbres Site In Southwestern New Mexico,* H.S. and
C.B. Cosgrove, Vol. XV, No. 1, Peabody Museum Of
American Archaeology And Ethnology.

PLATE 22   Bold flowing curved elements balanced by delicate areas of rhythmical straight lines combine to form an unusual geometric pattern.

after Plate 151, Figure e, *The Swarts Ruin: A Typical Mimbres Site In Southwestern New Mexico,* H.S. and C.B. Cosgrove, Vol. XV, No. 1, Peabody Museum Of American Archaeology And Ethnology.

PLATE 23   The innocent, childlike representation of this caterpillar—caught at the moment of contraction awaiting the slow forward surge—is an excellent example of the unhampered, carefree manner in which the Mimbres were able to approach nature.

after Plate 196, Figure f, *The Swarts Ruin: A Typical Mimbres Site In Southwestern New Mexico,* H.S. and C.B. Cosgrove, Vol. XV, No. 1, Peabody Museum Of American Archaeology And Ethnology.

PLATE 24   One of the rare animal forms embodying ferociousness, this naturalistic design of two mountain lions conveys an aura of impending danger. Not only
do the forward curved tails (which are a trait of Mimbres' mountain lions) portray
anger, but the geometric body designs give a feeling of confined energy waiting to
be unleashed. The cats are mean and ready to spring.

after Figure 12, *Additional Designs On Prehistoric
Mimbres Pottery*, J. Walter Fewkes, Smithsonian
Miscellaneous Collection, Vol. 76, No. 8, Smithsonian
Institution.

PLATE 25   *Vibrating sawtooth areas fade into graceful, undulating curves,
accented by fine uniform lines, the totality of which is a unified rhythmic design.
A masterful union of dissimilar geometric elements—another of the Mimbres
outstanding talents.*

after Plate 164, Figure b, *The Swarts Ruin: A Typical
Mimbres Site In Southwestern New Mexico,* H.S. and
C.B. Cosgrove, Vol. XV, No. 1, Peabody Museum Of
American Archaeology And Ethnology.

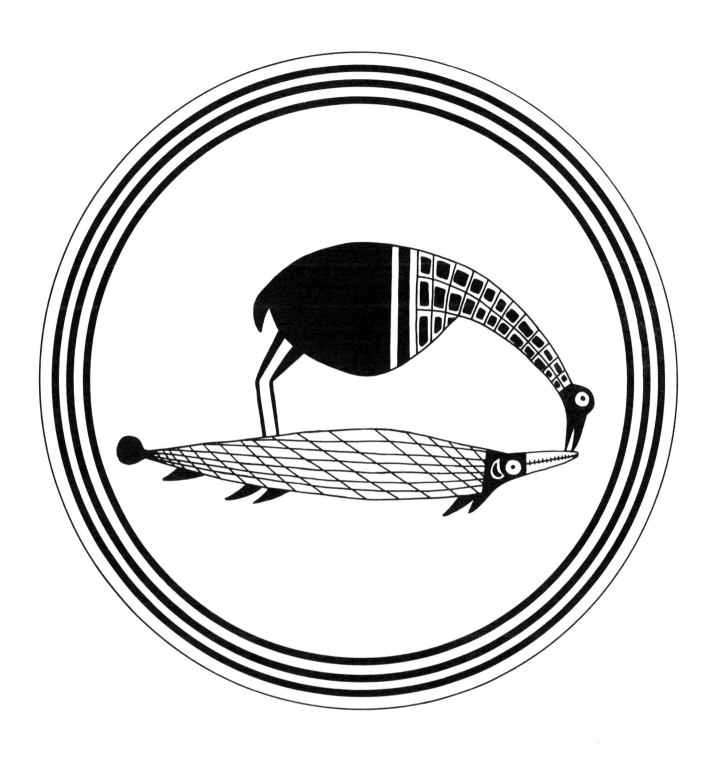

PLATE 26   *What were the Mimbres illustrating by having various animals connected mouth-to-mouth? Notice the irregular, casually placed lines—suggesting fish scales—that imply simplicity yet help develop the highly stylized character of this design.*

after Plate 209, Figure b, *The Swarts Ruin: A Typical Mimbres Site In Southwestern New Mexico,* H.S. and C.B. Cosgrove, Vol. XV, No. 1, Peabody Museum Of American Archaeology And Ethnology.

PLATE 27   Grasshoppers racing around the bowl? Is it the same grasshopper in slightly varying positions or different grasshoppers in each oval? The latter is probable as a careful look brings to light differences between each insect—but perhaps this is simply the results of the unmechanical hand-executed design.

after Figure 94, *Designs On Prehistoric Pottery From The Mimbres Valley, New Mexico,* J. Walter Fewkes, Smithsonian Miscellaneous Collection, Vol. 74, No. 6, Smithsonian Institution.

PLATE 28   Is it possible that the Mimbres were attempting to portray the natural
phenomena of plant growth radiating from a central axis? Even if the Mimbres
were not trying to illustrate such a profound concept, this design is one of the rare
instances in which plant forms are represented in Mimbres pottery. It may also be
that these seemingly flower-like forms were not meant to represent stylized
blossoms at all, but are merely one of the many varied geometric elements in
this design.

after Figure 112, *Designs On Prehistoric Pottery From
The Mimbres Valley, New Mexico,* J. Walter Fewkes,
Smithsonian Miscellaneous Collection, Vol. 74, No. 6,
Smithsonian Institution.

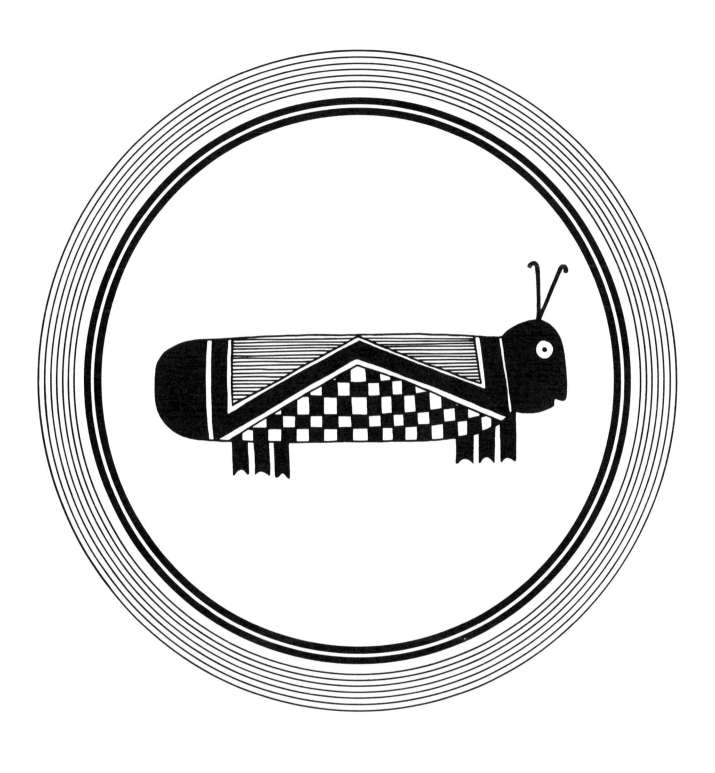

PLATE 29   *Not portrayed as the dreaded destroyer of crops and plant life, this childlike representation of a caterpillar carries with it a warm harmless aura. In images such as this, truly innocent qualities of the Mimbres art are felt—which are in sharp contrast to the sophistication of designs in Plates 12 and 20.*

after Figure 96, *Designs On Prehistoric Pottery From The Mimbres Valley, New Mexico,* J. Walter Fewkes, Smithsonian Miscellaneous Collection, Vol. 74, No. 6, Smithsonian Institution.

PLATE 30   *Harmonious coexistence or a piggyback ride on a whimsical creature?*
This design combines several of the reoccurring elements in Mimbres art. Most
evident in the design are the ill-proportioned, vaguely represented human forms
sharply contrasted against the gaily patterned animals. The Mimbres elaborately
adorned their animal figures, while illustrating themselves in very crude
undeveloped forms. Intermingling of naturalistic and geometric elements is an
additional Mimbres talent brought to light in this design.

after Figure 7, *Designs On Prehistoric Pottery From The*
Mimbres Valley, New Mexico, J. Walter Fewkes,
Smithsonian Miscellaneous Collection, Vol. 74, No. 6,
Smithsonian Institution.

PLATE 31   *Emerging from the sides of the bowl, the vividly patterned wolf not only*
is a complete image in itself but forms an integral part of the bowl's total design.
Visually the wolf and its elongated tail flow with the bowl's contour and painted
border, making it difficult to separate the two. Beyond simply painting an animal
figure in the bottom of a bowl, this unique design exemplifies the Mimbres' ability
to cleverly unify a naturalistic image with the structure of a bowl.

after Figure 10, *Additional Designs On Prehistoric*
Mimbres Pottery, J. Walter Fewkes, Smithsonian
Miscellaneous Collection, Vol. 76, No. 8, Smithsonian
Institution.

PLATE 32   *Have the projections from the sides of the bowl caused the coiling reflex of this millipedelike creature? The natural response of such an animal to coil when touched is graphically brought to mind by the protrusions of the background design which surround and imprison him.*

after Plate 196, Figure d, *The Swarts Ruin: A Typical Mimbres Site In Southwestern New Mexico*, H.S. and C.B. Cosgrove, Vol. XV, No. 1, Peabody Museum Of American Archaeology And Ethnology.

PLATE 33   *Energy exploding from an inner core while simultaneously being driven inward by the intrusion of the wedge-shaped checkerboards charge this geometric design with turbulent excitement. Could this energy be the Mimbres interpretation of natural forces, such as the sparks created when smashing stones together, or is this a geometric design for design sake only?*

after Plate 141, Figure a, *The Swarts Ruin: A Typical Mimbres Site In Southwestern New Mexico,* H.S. and C.B. Cosgrove, Vol. XV, No. 1, Peabody Museum Of American Archaeology And Ethnology.

PLATE 34   *A pinwheel motif, with careful observation, becomes a design
ingeniously devised by the union of insectlike animals. Masters of mixing design
elements, the Mimbres continually created forms that can be appreciated in their
totality as well as for their separate parts, as in this design.*

after Figure 119, *Designs On Prehistoric Pottery From
The Mimbres Valley, New Mexico,* J. Walter Fewkes,
Smithsonian Miscellaneous Collection, Vol. 74, No. 6,
Smithsonian Institution.

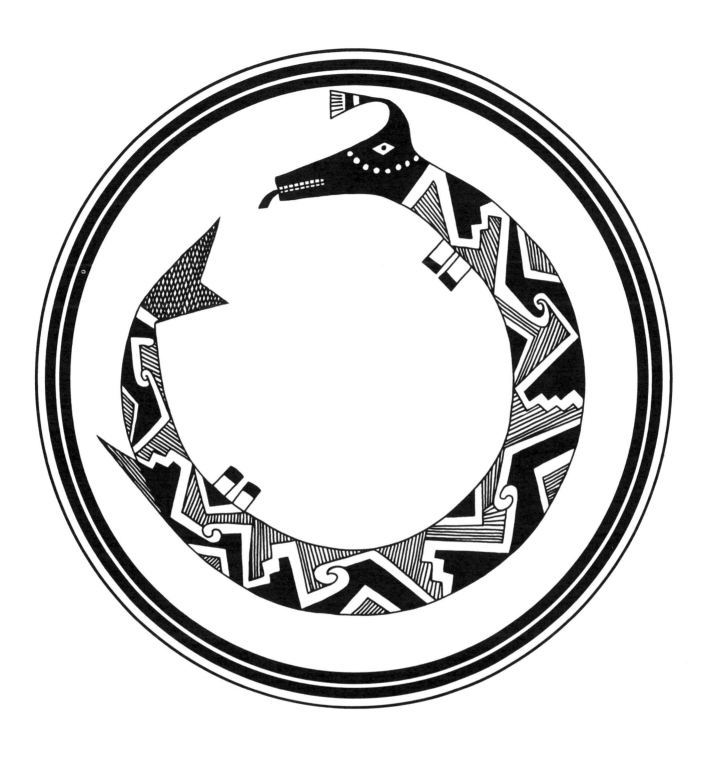

PLATE 35   *Were the Mimbres plagued by tobacco worms (also called southern hornworms) as farmers of today, or is the boldly decorated creature a product of an imaginative mind combining various features of different animals? That the tobacco worm was a concern of the Mimbres is very possible as it voraciously eats the leaves of tobacco, tomato and potato plants—all of which are indigenous to the New World. Plate 29 is also reminiscent of a tobacco worm (larvae of the sphinx moth).*

after Figure 41, *Designs On Prehistoric Pottery From The Mimbres Valley, New Mexico,* J. Walter Fewkes, Smithsonian Miscellaneous Collection, Vol. 74, No. 6, Smithsonian Institution.

PLATE 36   Skillful dexterity and imaginative combinations of asymmetry and negative images are highlighted by this elaborate geometric design. The deft brushstrokes carry the eye smoothly through the design which is almost a mirror-image in a positive and negative form, the black areas being mirrored by similar areas of carefully placed fine lines. Also, positive and negative images flow in and out of each other, creating a total design unit rather than one separated by its parts.

after Plate 133, Figure e, *The Swarts Ruin: A Typical Mimbres Site In Southwestern New Mexico*, H.S. and C.B. Cosgrove, Vol. XV, No. 1, Peabody Museum Of American Archaeology And Ethnology.

PLATE 37   Beavers? These animals are almost mirror images of each other, yet the protruding noses differ greatly. The concentric circular motion gives the feeling that the animals are rotating inside the bowl or perhaps chasing each other.

after Figure 19, *Designs On Prehistoric Pottery From The Mimbres Valley, New Mexico,* J. Walter Fewkes, Smithsonian Miscellaneous Collection, Vol. 74, No. 6, Smithsonian Institution.

PLATE 38   An insect kiss—or simply two bugs joined for the sake of design? Note
the stark white background as compared to the ornate background of Plate 37,
again another example of the limitless versatility displayed by the Mimbres.

after Plate 192, Figure e, *The Swarts Ruin: A Typical*
Mimbres Site In Southwestern New Mexico, H.S. and
C.B. Cosgrove, Vol. XV, No. 1, Peabody Museum Of
American Archaeology And Ethnology.

PLATE 39   *Triplicity of geometric elements give this round design a triangular dimension.*

after Plate 146, Figure f, *The Swarts Ruin: A Typical Mimbres Site In Southwestern New Mexico,* H.S. and C.B. Cosgrove, Vol. XV, No. 1, Peabody Museum Of American Archaeology And Ethnology.

PLATE 40   Pushing at the edge of the bowl, the ram stands captured in a moment of forward surging energy. Adding to the frenzied character of the ram are the abrupt irregular border projections which seem to prod him on.

after Plate 221, Figure a, *The Swarts Ruin: A Typical Mimbres Site In Southwestern New Mexico,* H.S. and C.B. Cosgrove, Vol. XV, No. 1, Peabody Museum Of American Archaeology And Ethnology.